Greater Than a Tourist
Book Series
Reviews from Readers

I think the series is wonderful and beneficial for tourists to get information before visiting the city.

-Seckin Zumbul, Izmir Turkey

I am a world traveler who has read many trip guides but this one really made a difference for me. I would call it a heartfelt creation of a local guide expert instead of just a guide.

-Susy, Isla Holbox, Mexico

New to the area like me, this is a must have!

-Joe, Bloomington, USA

This is a good series that gets down to it when looking for things to do at your destination without having to read a novel for just a few ideas.

-Rachel, Monterey, USA

Good information to have to plan my trip to this destination.

-Pennie Farrell, Mexico

Great ideas for a port day.

-Mary Martin USA

Aptly titled, you won't just be a tourist after reading this book. You'll be greater than a tourist!

-Alan Warner, Grand Rapids, USA

Even though I only have three days to spend in San Miguel in an upcoming visit, I will use the author's suggestions to guide some of my time there. An easy read - with chapters named to guide me in directions I want to go.

-Robert Catapano, USA

Great insights from a local perspective! Useful information and a very good value!

-Sarah, USA

This series provides an in-depth experience through the eyes of a local. Reading these series will help you to travel the city in with confidence and it'll make your journey a unique one.

-Andrew Teoh, Ipoh, Malaysia

GREATER THAN A TOURIST- MANCHESTER UNITED KINGDOM

50 Travel Tips from a Local

Adam Fraiel

First Edition

Cover designed by: Ivana Stamenkovic

Cover Image: By Mark Andrew. - Manchester town hall., CC BY 2.0,
https://commons.wikimedia.org/w/index.php?curid=23213538

Images:

1. https://en.wikipedia.org/wiki/File:Piccadilly_Station_Manchester_-
geograph.org.uk-_692981.jpg

2. https://en.wikipedia.org/wiki/File:Etihad_Stadium.jpg

3.
https://en.wikipedia.org/wiki/File:Manchester_United_Panorama_(8051523746).
jpg

4. https://en.wikipedia.org/wiki/File:Canal_street_manchester.jpg

CZYK Publishing Since 2011.
CZYKPublishing.com
Greater Than a Tourist

Lock Haven, PA
All rights reserved.
ISBN: 9798465846134

>TOURIST

50 TRAVEL TIPS FROM A LOCAL

BOOK DESCRIPTION

With travel tips and culture in our guidebooks written by a local, it is never too late to visit Manchester. Greater Than a Tourist- Manchester, UK by Author Adam Fraiel offers the inside scoop on Cottonopolis. Most travel books tell you how to travel like a tourist. Although there is nothing wrong with that, as part of the 'Greater Than a Tourist' series, this book will give you candid travel tips from someone who has lived at your next travel destination. This guide book will not tell you exact addresses or store hours but instead gives you knowledge that you may not find in other smaller print travel books. Experience cultural, culinary delights, and attractions with the guidance of a Local. Slow down and get to know the people with this invaluable guide. By the time you finish this book, you will be eager and prepared to discover new activities at your next travel destination.

Inside this travel guide book you will find:

Visitor information from a Local
Tour ideas and inspiration
Save time with valuable guidebook information

Greater Than a Tourist- A Travel Guidebook with 50 Travel Tips from a Local. Slow down, stay in one place, and get to know the people and culture. By the time you finish this book, you will be eager and prepared to travel to your next destination.

OUR STORY

Traveling is a passion of the Greater than a Tourist book series creator. Lisa studied abroad in college, and for their honeymoon Lisa and her husband toured Europe. During her travels to Malta, an older man tried to give her some advice based on his own experience living on the island since he was a young boy. She was not sure if she should talk to the stranger but was interested in his advice. When traveling to some places she was wary to talk to locals because she was afraid that they weren't being genuine. Through her travels, Lisa learned how much locals had to share with tourists. Lisa created the Greater Than a Tourist book series to help connect people with locals. A topic that locals are very passionate about sharing.

TABLE OF CONTENTS

DEDICATION

This book is dedicated to my Mum and Dad, Pat and Frank. Without their unwavering support and bottomless pool of love, I wouldn't have accomplished a fraction of my dreams.

Is breá liom leat chun an ghealach agus ar ais

ABOUT THE AUTHOR

Adam Fraiel was born and bred in Manchester and, although he's been travelling off and on for most of his adult life, he always returns to basecamp. An award-nominated blogger, published author and now professional copywriter, his work allows him the opportunity to wander whenever possible.

When not being kidnapped by Costa Rican cowboys or falling off mountains, he likes to swing his kettlebells and strum his ukulele.

You can follow his wanderings on Instagram @allaboardthefraytrain

HOW TO USE THIS BOOK

The *Greater Than a Tourist* book series was written by someone who has lived in an area for over three months. The goal of this book is to help travelers either dream or experience different locations by providing opinions from a local. The author has made suggestions based on their own experiences. Please check before traveling to the area in case the suggested places are unavailable.

Travel Advisories: As a first step in planning any trip abroad, check the Travel Advisories for your intended destination.
https://travel.state.gov/content/travel/en/traveladvisories/traveladvisories.html

FROM THE PUBLISHER

Traveling can be one of the most important parts of a person's life. The anticipation and memories that you have are some of the best. As a publisher of the Greater Than a Tourist, as well as the popular *50 Things to Know* book series, we strive to help you learn about new places, spark your imagination, and inspire you. Wherever you are and whatever you do I wish you safe, fun, and inspiring travel.

Lisa Rusczyk Ed. D.
CZYK Publishing

WELCOME TO
> TOURIST

Manchester Piccadilly Station

The Etihad Stadium is home to Premier League club Manchester City FC

Old Trafford is home to Premier League club Manchester United

Canal Street, one of Manchester's liveliest nightspots, part of the city's gay village

"Life is like riding a bicycle. To keep your balance, you must keep moving."

Albert Einstein

Manchester's a funny old city. It's been at the centre of some of the greatest developments in human history - the Industrial Revolution, the Suffragette movement and splitting the atom. That's not including all the sporting and musical accomplishments.

Yet, with all that history, I know plenty of Mancunians who are baffled that anyone would ever want to visit. I was the same. The more I travelled, the more people would ask about Manchester, and how great it was.

For me, the grass was always greener, so I never took the time to explore what was on my doorstep.

Manchester, like the locals, is fairly unassuming. It's not brash or particularly in your face. It's no-nonsense, practical and quite self-effacing.

You could quite easily walk through the city and miss 90% of the 'attractions'. A few old buildings here, a shopping centre there. I made that mistake for most of my adult life.

It was only after travelling the world for years that I returned and truly discovered it myself. I made a mindset shift and began looking at Manchester with the same curiosity and excitement I give to foreign lands.

I loved what I found.

Manchester
UK

Manchester United Kingdom Climate

	High	Low
January	45	35
February	45	35
March	50	37
April	54	40
May	61	45
June	65	50
July	69	54
August	68	53
September	63	49
October	57	45
November	50	39
December	46	36

GreaterThanaTourist.com

Temperatures are in Fahrenheit degrees.
Source: NOAA

1. START IN THE CENTRE

If you've only got a few days to explore Manchester, I recommend starting in the centre and working your way out.

Slap bang in the middle of town is where you'll find Manchester Town Hall. A fine place to start!

Finished in 1877, it was designed to rival the best London had to offer. While it may not be as vast as Westminster Abbey or The Houses of Parliament, it's still a very impressive building. The neo-gothic architecture has a real Harry Potter vibe - dark and menacing, yet with a hint of magic.

What a lot of locals aren't aware of is that you're allowed in, and it's free! You get to wander around the grade 1 listed building, admiring the dark, brooding interior. Don't be surprised if you hear wedding bells too. It's a popular venue, and not too expensive considering the location.

The square outside, Albert Square, is the home to several festivals and events throughout the year. The biggest is easily the Christmas Markets, running from November to the end of December. While they snake out to cover the entire city centre, Albert Square is the heart.

Whenever you're visiting, it's always worth paying a visit to the square. You might catch a free concert, join in with a political rally or stuff your face at a random food festival.

2. READING IS WHAT? FUNDAMENTAL

I'm not sure if it's a coincidence, but a lot of the beautiful buildings in Manchester are libraries.

From Albert Square, head straight down Brazennose Street (one of my favourite street names) and you'll come out on Deansgate. Right in front of you will be another dark, imposing gothic building. That is John Rylands Library.

For years I walked past it, always wondering yet never knowing what went on inside. The front 'entrance' isn't used. It's blocked up and gives no welcoming vibes at all.

Ignore that! Go round the side. There'll you'll find a shiny glass entrance and lovely welcoming staff. It's completely free to enter and it'll blow your mind.

If you thought the Town Hall was Potter-esque, you'll live your wizarding fantasy in John Rylands.

Built in 1900 in honour of her late husband (and Manchester's first millionaire), Mrs Enriqueta Rylands wanted something that would benefit the community while looking fabulous. It does both.

What people may not be aware of is that, at certain points of the year, it stops being a spooky old building and becomes… an even spookier building. Around Halloween time it plays host to movie nights, usually showing the old classics.

It's recommended to get wrapped up warm, as Manchester in November can be chilly. Plus the blanket gives you something to hide beneath if it all gets a bit too scary.

3. THE MUSIC SCHOOL THAT LAUNCHED THE COMMUNIST MANIFESTO

Yet another fabulous free Manchester library is Chethams. More commonly known by the locals as Chethams School of Music, there's also a library hidden there. Again, it's set back and doesn't have any big welcome signs, but it's a must while you're on the history tour.

How old is it? It's only the oldest free public reference library in the English-speaking world, operating since 1653.

As with John Rylands, it's a functioning library, so you're free to sit and study here. The combination of the ancient works, medieval surroundings and ambience cannot be put into words. If you need some quiet time away from the city centre, either of these are fabulous options.

Booking on a tour will reveal the communist connection. You'll see the exact room and desk where Karl Marx and Friedrich Engels worked back in 1845. Their research together during this time eventually led to the writing of the Communist Manifesto.

4. KEEP GOING BACK

Keeping the history vibe going, let's go back a little further... to the Romans.

Head straight down Deansgate for 10 minutes and you'll come to an area called Castlefield. It's here you can see 3 very distinct stages of Manchester history.

Discovered only as recently as 100 years ago, ancient Roman foundations have been uncovered and reconstructed. A fort, dating back to 79 AD, called Mancunium (hence where the name for people from Manchester, Mancunians, came from).

While wandering through the ruins you also see vestiges of The Industrial Revolution - cotton mills, warehouses and the all-important rivers that run through Manchester. More on those later.

Finally, you see the latest stage in Manchester's evolution - the redevelopment and reinvestment.

Castlefield Bowl is home to a superb yearly music festival, featuring huge international acts such as Snow Patrol, Lewis Capaldi and Crowded House.

Sinking a frosty pint of beer in the late Manchester sunshine, fine music blasting out and ancient history all around… it can be a little surreal.

5. FOLLOW THE RIVER

The rivers I mentioned earlier were the key to Manchester's success oh so many years ago. 3 rivers flow through the city - The Irwell, Irk and Medlock.

These rivers, combined with the Bridgewater Canal, hand-dug and completed in 1761, marked the beginning of the Industrial Revolution and catapulted Manchester to the centre of the action.

You can still see the mills and industrial footprint, although nowadays most have been converted to fancy 'riverside' apartments.

With these apartments came bars and restaurants looking out on the water and, on a sunny day with your eyes closed tight and your imagination running, you could almost believe you were somewhere abroad.

I highly recommend taking a walk down the canals. If you were adventurous you could wander for miles, ending up way outside the city centre in any direction.

6. INTO THE FUTURE

While we're still in the city centre, back up a little from Castlefield and head to Liverpool Road. Here we find The Science and Industry Museum. Admittedly, the name sounds a little dry, but it's amazing! Trust me.

Built on the site of the world's oldest surviving passenger railway station, they strike a fantastic balance between the ancient and forgotten with modern, contemporary science.

It's not a passive experience. Yes, there are exhibitions to see and information to read, but the real magic comes with so many interactive elements. If you're no longer a child, prepare to regress!

The exhibitions range from vehicles to the human body to robots and space. If you have even the slightest curiosity about how things work, you'll be like a pig in muck! (that's a positive)

The best part? It's free! You'll need to reserve your spot via their website, but it won't cost you anything.

7. MANCHESTER MUSEUM

Manchester Museum is a little more orthodox with traditional exhibitions, but it's still phenomenal.

It's a little journey out of the city centre, either a 30-minute walk or 5 minutes on the bus straight up Oxford Road. It's worth the trip and should absolutely be on your itinerary.

Yet another neo-gothic beast of a building, it's housed plenty of world-famous exhibitions. The most memorable was all about the ancient Egyptian culture. So popular did it become that it then went on a world tour, but it shall return!

They handle ancient cultures, natural curiosities and also plenty of thought-provoking exhibits, linking the past to our modern lives. It's also home to Stan, the resident T-Rex. He's worth a visit alone.

You guessed it - free! As with the Science and Industry Museum, book in advance, but yet again just a formality.

8. MANCHESTER AND THE SUFFRAGETTE MOVEMENT

Carry on a little further up, 5 minutes walk max, and you come to Manchester Royal Infirmary. No, I'm not including a hospital in this guide. I'd be getting really desperate for sites if I did.

Across the road from the hospital you'll see a row of brick houses. They stand out alongside the glass monstrosity of the hospital, yet if you didn't know what they were, you'd easily ignore them.

I worked at that very hospital for years and never knew what they were.

Turns out it's the most important historical site with regards to women's suffrage and the launch of the suffrage movement. Now called The Pankhurst Centre after Emmeline Pankhurst, it's the only museum dedicated to telling the story of women's right to vote.

Although it was finalised in London, it all started here in Manchester.

Entry is free, although donations are welcomed to help with the upkeep and maintenance,

9. MANCHESTER ART GALLERY

Back in town now and a tour of Manchester wouldn't be complete without popping into Manchester Art Gallery. Set back on Mosely Street, it's a stone's throw from the Town Hall.

Yet again, free to enter, I've wandered these halls more times than I can remember.

I could stand and stare at Wagner's 'The Chariot Race' all day long and never grow tired.

Classic paintings, sculptures and historical artefacts are the order of the day. If you're an art lover, it's a dream.

A recent addition was their virtual gallery, which I think's a pretty good idea. They admitted they could only physically display around 3% of their vast back catalogue, so they put it all on virtual-display. Check out their website for the full catalogue.

10. CENTRAL LIBRARY

The final stop on the museum/library tour is a 30-second walk from Manchester Art Gallery, standing adjacent to The Town Hall.

Central Library is an iconic landmark in the city centre. Inspired by the Pantheon in Rome, it certainly stands out. Whereas almost everything else in the city is square or straight lines, this circular beauty is a breath of fresh air.

It recently underwent a multi-year restoration project, alongside the square in front - St Peter's Square.

I spent most of my adult life believing the square was just a square, until I discovered it was the site of a massacre! They don't advertise that in the brochures.

Back in 1819, the peasants were unhappy with life. Unemployment was rife and they weren't entitled to vote. A crowd of 60,000 gathered in St Peter's Square (then St Peter's Field) and demanded political reform. The rich folk didn't agree and so sent in the cavalry.

Charging in with sabres drawn, 18 died and several hundred were injured.

Did they get their reform? Absolutely. The government swiftly passed The Six Acts, preventing any future gatherings with the intent of political reform. Another win for the ruling elite.

A monument now stands in the square - a mound made up of 11 concentric circles. It's easy to walk over it without ever knowing the significance, so I hope this helped fill in a few gaps.

11. FANCY A SPOT OF SHOPPING?

If shopping's your thing, Manchester's your place. Depending on what you're looking for and your budget, you've got plenty of options.

The classic shopping destination in the city centre is The Arndale. It's vast and covers most bases - food, fashion and entertainment, all housed under one roof.

It's mostly circular so you can't get lost, although it can be a little disorienting if it's your first time. Spanning two floors, you can easily spend a few hours wandering. Mostly budget or mid-range items, there are still some high-end fashion shops to choose from.

12. HIT THE ARCADES

If money's no object then you'll want to head south down Deansgate. Here you'll find Kendals and House of Fraser, along with the beautiful Barton Arcade.

You could easily pass by and miss it, but wandering inside you'll be treated to a masterclass in glass and iron. Dating back to 1871, it's a time capsule for Victorian Manchester. On a sunny day, the glass atrium is heavenly. On a not so sunny day, it's a perfect little spot to escape the rain, grab a coffee and dry out.

While the shops in the city are always evolving, The Barton Arcade features plenty of pop-up shops - a Christmas Mulled Wine bar being my personal favourite. The local indie brands or quirky bars complement the bigger, more established labels and it all just flows.

For years the arcade was just a cut-through to get from Deansgate to St Ann's Square behind, but with all the love, care and restoration that's been put in, it's now a must-visit spot in the city centre.

13. GO FOR A BIG SHOP

If you're serious about shopping, you'll have to take a detour out of the city centre and take the Metrolink to The Trafford Centre. It'll take around 20 minutes to get there, and the rest of the day to explore the vast complex.

Spanning over 200,000m2 and boasting design inspiration from the Titanic, The Vatican and Las Vegas, it's a sight to behold.

200 shops attract over 30 million customers per year. High fashion, tech and healthcare are just a sample of what you'll find. If, for some crazy reason, you get bored of shopping, you can try 18-holes of mini-golf, 10-pin bowling or ride dodgem cars. Did I mention Legoland and Sea Life are also on-site?

It's vast!

There are also plenty of places to grab a snack, but we'll cover that shortly.

If you can't take a quality selfie here, be it with one of the biggest chandeliers in the world, a dome bigger than that in St. Paul's Cathedral or any of the random pop-up events (beaches, fun fares or F1 race tracks), hang up your camera.

14. HEAD TO THE NORTH

If the idea of millions of shoppers scares you a little, come back to town and wander over to the Northern Quarter. Once one of the most miserable and dangerous parts of the city, years of investment and renovation have turned it into a hipster's paradise.

Retro, quirky, alternative - they all fit when describing this area of town.

Where the Arndale and Trafford Centre are mainstream, this maze of side streets and alleys is home to independent boutiques, weird gadget shops and unique bars.

Two iconic locations you have to visit are Manchester Craft and Design Centre, and Affleck's Palace.

The Craft and Design Centre is set back and easily missable. Formerly a fish market, it's now home to multiple little studios for local designers, artists and crafty folk to sell their wares directly to the public. If you're after an unusual and unique gift idea, this is a great place to start.

With two floors of handmade jewellery, paintings or ceramics, the artists are always welcoming and chatty. Watch as they create the next batch of accessories, or paint incredible landscapes. If you're a creative person, you'll connect with the amazing energy in the centre.

Affleck's Palace is a completely different beast. Jam-packed with retro, vintage and pre-loved (a fancy name for second-hand) items, you really never know what you'll find. Memorabilia, fashion and weird shops that don't fit any bracket will keep you entertained for a good while as you explore the 4 floors.

If you've got a fancy dress party coming up, Affleck's is the dream location!

15. A TRIP TO THE BEECH

30 minutes south on the Metrolink will take you to Chorlton. While the shopping area is relatively small, it's a welcome break from the hustle of the city centre. The area's renowned as an alternative/hipster/bohemian part of Manchester.

Wander from the Chorlton Bookshop to Tiny's Tipple bottle shop to Furcats Cat Boutique. Those 3 shops should cover all potential gift ideas, all in the space of a few feet.

If it's sunny, head down to Beech Road and enjoy a frosty beverage in one of the many excellent pubs and bars. If you stick around for the nightlife, you won't be disappointed. Whatever your choice of entertainment, you'll likely find it in Chorlton.

Open mic stand-up, live music and chilled cocktail bars are all available. If you want to dance, rock out or have a good laugh, you could do much worse than pay a visit to Chorlton.

16. HUNGRY FELLA? HERE YOU GO

If all that talk of shopping has made you a bit peckish, you've got options.

As with the shopping recommendations, it all depends on your budget and the time of day. If its during the daytime, the Arndale is a decent option.

On one end there's a giant food court, featuring all the classic fast-food takeaways - McDonald's, Subway, KFC etc. On the opposite side is the Food Market. That's another world, housing kiosks selling foods from Jamaican to Italian, and everything in between.

I'd personally recommend the Food Market. It's real food and normally much cheaper, although each to their own.

The combination of smells can get a little overwhelming in such a compact space, and the surrounding stalls - mobile phones, discount shoes and costume jewellery don't always lend themselves to a calm eating environment. But it's tasty food at a great price.

17. YOU SPIN ME RIGHT ROUND

If you're after fine-dining, go to Spinningfields. After over £1Billion of investment, it's the 'Canary Wharf of the North' - the giant glass financial district of Manchester. While that may not sound like the best place to grab a meal, you'd be surprised.

Here you'll find luxury brands like Emporio Armani, Mulberry and Flannels. You'll also find some of the city's most exclusive bars and restaurants. Frequented by local celebrities, you'll need to get dressed up if you want to get in.

With a choice of exotic Asian restaurants, Italian street food or Brazilian classics, I'd personally recommend a place called Bill's. It may not have the most exciting name, but the food makes up for it in spades. The British classics are worth every penny, plus they also offer excellent plant-based alternatives.

After eating, head to any one of the rooftop terrace bars for a view of Manchester by night. Not quite Vegas, but still quite pretty.

18. A SPICY TWIST

If glass and chrome (and huge food bills) aren't your thing, travel to another world by heading south. Only 20 minutes outside the city centre, Levenshulme is a delight for the senses.

One of the most diverse areas of Manchester, you'll find so much great food here. Restaurants sitting side by side offering everything from Lebanese to Jamaican, and Thai to classic English tea rooms.

I love driving down Stockport Road on a Friday evening. On one hand, it's a nightmare due to traffic, but just roll down the windows and appreciate a hundred different smells and aromas.

Without a doubt, go to New Himalayas. No hesitation or doubts. If you like curry, I doubt you could find a better one in the city. If it's cold outside, the warmth and friendliness of the staff will thaw you out. Vegetarian? They've got you covered. I'm not much of a foodie, but this place I'll sing about from the rafters.

Aside from the fine food, Levenshulme (or Levy for short) is known for its amazing community spirit.

33

There's no better example than the weekend community market. There's a big emphasis on ethical and eco-friendly goods, and it's all served with a smile. If you're in Manchester between March and December, add it to your itinerary.

19. BACK TO THE TRAFFORD CENTRE

As I mentioned earlier, the Trafford Centre is a huge complex with something for everyone. That's also the case with food. It's home to the biggest food court in Europe, seating 1600 diners.

You've got a choice from around 50 different outlets, split between fast food and sit-down restaurants. Name a style of food and you'll likely find it here (they even have a Bill's). Catering for all budgets and hunger levels, you won't go hungry in the Trafford Centre.

Aside from the actual food, the surroundings really make it. The majority of the restaurants are located in an area called The Orient. Remember earlier how I mentioned themes like the Vatican and Las Vegas? The Orient goes for a more early 1900s cruise liner. While you're waiting for your food, be sure to look up. The vast ceiling lighting changes to mimic the different stages of the day, from bright sunshine to stars at night.

While it's not an experience I'd make a habit of, it's certainly unique.

20. ESCAPE TO THE ISLAND

One of the newest additions to the Manchester line-up, Escape to Freight Island came in swinging! Located just a few minutes walk from the main train station, Manchester Piccadilly, it's an oasis in the urban jungle.

Built on the site of an abandoned freight train depot, it's now the city's biggest outdoor dining space. Bars, restaurants, open-air or covered, you'll be spoilt for choice.

Is it a fantastic space for meeting friends, enjoying delicious food and partying the night away? Absolutely. Would it be fun in the depths of a Manchester winter as you're struggling to feel your toes? Who's to say. I can say that it's well worth exploring and sampling all the delights on offer.

It's close enough to the centre that walking's no problem, but far enough away to help you forget you're in a concrete jungle.

21. MADCHESTER, THE MUSIC CAPITAL

Chances are you know Manchester music because of Oasis. Fair play, you're not wrong. However, dig a little deeper and you'll find Manchester's fingerprint on many of the musical scenes that swept the world.

In the 60s:

* The Hollies

* Herman's Hermits

* 10cc

While Liverpool was stealing most of the spotlight, the Mancs were still producing pop classics. Did you know the BeeGees started their career in Manchester?

70s-80s:

* Morrissey and The Smiths

* Joy Division

* Factory Records and the Hacienda

This list could go on forever with the Happy Mondays, Buzzcocks, The Fall, 808state and many more. Thankfully there's a superb exhibition in The

Science and Industry Museum which covers this
glorious age of music.

90s onward:

- Stone Roses

- Oasis

- The Verve

Other unforgettable anthems came from James, The
Charlatans, Courteeners, Elbow and Doves. This was
the music of my youth… a fine time to be alive
indeed.

While it's not the music powerhouse it once was,
there are still plenty of great bands doing the local
scene. And there's no shortage of venues to catch live
music in the city.

22. NIGHT AND DAY

Small and unassuming, you could easily pass it on
Oldham Street, completely unaware of the history and
epic bands who've passed through on their way to
global stardom.

Bands such as Kasabian, Paulo Nutini and The Arctic Monkeys have all paid their dues in this iconic venue.

It's evolved over the years, from a chip shop back in the 90s to the current venue. It's not the biggest stage, but the atmosphere's special indeed. If you've got an evening spare, get in there. Tickets are cheap, and you could be seeing an early performance from the next stadium headliners.

Don't be surprised if you make some new friends and end up on a pub crawl across the city afterwards. Everyone's in there for a good time, so ride the wave and enjoy the evening.

If, for some reason, you don't fancy the bands that night, pop next door to The Dry Bar for an alternative selection of live music. You'll be spoiled for choice.

23. THE APOLLO

I've had some of the best musical experiences of my life in that building.

You'll find mid-level, established and alternate bands here, and it's an amazing venue! With a 3500 capacity, tiered seating upstairs gives an awesome view, or get stuck into the action in the downstairs standing section.

Wherever you are, there's a level of intimacy and connection you won't find at a stadium gig, but with stadium-quality bands. Slash, Alice Cooper, Neil Young, Tool, The Flaming Lips - they've all rocked my world in The Apollo.

You'll want to book tickets in advance as most shows sell out, and tickets outside can be silly prices.

It's also a superb venue to watch comedy shows. If a famous comedian is touring, they'll be playing The Apollo. The downstairs converts to fully seating, and there's not a bad seat in the house.

24. BAND ON THE WALL

Another iconic Manchester music venue, with this one able to trace its roots back to the 1930s. Frequented by foreign servicemen and local millworkers, they'd play on through the air-raid sirens on World War II in an act of defiance.

Plenty of the Manchester legends cut their teeth there, from the Buzzcocks to Joy Division. It's got a rich history of presenting famous bands, but they also have a great community spirit. With courses and music classes running year-round, they're helping to nurture tomorrow's talent.

After several renovations and upgrades, it's a superb venue for all forms of entertainment. If you're in town and don't mind what you see, it's always worth checking their eclectic listings.

25. ALL THE REST

It's easy to become complacent and take all the live music for granted. Having lived in several countries around the world, not everywhere has that opportunity. Not everywhere has such a deep talent pool playing 7 nights a week.

If you're visiting Manchester, take advantage and go see some gigs. There are hundreds of venues scattered around the city, from dirty old pubs to 21,000-seater arenas. On any given night in the city, you'll be able to find someone playing.

Other fine music venues include:

- The Deaf Institute
- Manchester Academy 1,2 and 3

- Albert Hall

- The Bridgewater Hall

- The Stoller Hall

26. THE ELEPHANT IN THE ROOM - FOOTBALL

"You're from Manchester? Are you a red or blue?"

That's without doubt the number 1 question I'm asked whenever I mention my roots. The truth is, I don't much care for football, but it wouldn't be much of a Manchester guide without talking about 'the beautiful game'.

The city is home to 2 giants - Manchester United and Manchester City. If you have a clear favourite, I'd advise sticking to that side of town. There are plenty of 'red pubs' and 'blue pubs', so it's best to ask before whipping out your football shirt and rattle.

If you're a United fan head over to Stretford and the "The Theatre of Dreams", Old Trafford.

One thing to note: if you're getting a taxi or following a map, make sure you get the right Old Trafford. You may be disappointed if you turn up at the cricket stadium of the same name.

Tours of the stadium and museum run on non-match days. It lasts just over an hour and should provide enough selfie material to keep your feed nice and red.

If you wanted to make it an unforgettable experience you could sail to the stadium on a barge. Travel down the Manchester canal aboard The Princess Katherine before being dropped off right at the gate. It even takes you back once the game ends. It beats queuing for a Metrolink for 40 minutes.

27. THE BLUE SIDE OF TOWN

Manchester City reside over on the east side of town, in the Etihad Stadium. The Metrolink takes you directly there from the city centre, stopping right outside at the City Square stop.

As they're bitter rivals they obviously have to outdo United, so their tour takes approximately 90 minutes, and claims to be "the most immersive tour experience in Premier League Football".

For a little extra you can also tour the nearby Academy and HQ. Considering I'm not a big football fan, I must admit the facilities are impressive. Along with Old Trafford, the Etihad Stadium also features live concerts (Metallica, Foo Fighters, Spice Girls etc).

If you can time your trip to take in a concert there, you'll be a happy bunny indeed. Both are incredible music venues.

Within walking distance of the stadium, you'll also find The Manchester Velodrome, National Cycling Centre, National Indoor BMX Centre and National Squash Centre. It's a hotbed of activity and well worth exploring. If you want to get involved you can even book a session at the BMX centre.

28. THE FOOTBALL MUSEUM

If you still need more football in your life, visit the National Football Museum in the city centre. Entrance is free for Manchester residents, so try and find a local friend to experience it with.

There's the classic 'history of football' section which takes you from the old 'pig skin' days up to the modern game. There are also more interactive elements, where you get to test your penalty taking skills.

Then there's all the memorabilia and kits to satisfy your photographic needs. Pose with the trophies and admire the kits of old.

Depending on your love of the game, be prepared to spend anywhere from 2 to 4 hours exploring.

29. THE OTHER OLD TRAFFORD

As I mentioned before, there are 2 Old Traffords in Manchester - the football stadium and the cricket ground (The Emirates Old Trafford). If you've never been to a cricket game, consider it.

While the stereotype is old men falling asleep while clutching their thermos flask, the modern game can be quite exciting. The longer 5-day test matches may still be a little sleepy, there are plenty of T20 games throughout the year. These are much shorter, faster, feature players smashing the ball and have their own pyrotechnics.

Mexican waves are common, as are fancy dress and beer consumption. If you've got preconceptions about a typical cricket game, prepare to have them dashed. It's a lot of fun, and you can finally tick it off your bucketlist.

The Emirates Old Trafford is around a 20-minute walk from the football stadium, but it's right next to a Metrolink station. This makes getting to and from the ground simple. The stop is called Old Trafford.

If you can't watch a cricket game there, it also doubles as a fine concert venue. Beyonce, Foo

Fighters and David Bowie all played there, so keep an eye out and try to time your visit.

30. GO FOR A SWIM

Remember the canals we spoke of? Fancy swimming in them?

If you want bragging rights to say you lived the true Manchester experience, you have to go for a swim at Dock Nine, Salford Quays.

The venue for the 2002 Commonwealth Games, the company Uswim run sessions either Saturday morning or Wednesday evening. The water temperature can vary depending on the time of year, but let's just say it can be a little chilly.

Wetsuits are available to hire, and even compulsory when it gets too cold. The professional staff and guides take your safety very seriously, which should be reassuring.

Even better than a random swim would be to sign up for the Great Manchester Swim held in May. 3 miles, all timed with a chip and a medal at the end? What better Manchester souvenir than that?

There's usually a party atmosphere throughout, so even if you want to stay dry, it's worth heading down for the carnival spirit.

31. THE SUN GOING DOWN ON ME.

While you're in Salford Quays, consider sticking around for the sunset. After the redevelopment in the area, the cleaning of the waters and the building of Media City, the Quays are a beautiful place to hang out.

The sunsets there can be spectacular. There aren't many spots in the city centre that offer such views - the light bouncing from the water and the unique skyline, so make sure you've got your camera handy. They're not consistent, but you usually get a few epic evenings around late summer, in August/September.

If the evening's a dud then head across the Millenium Bridge to The Quays, another shopping complex, where you can enjoy a show at The Lowry Theatre, a walk around the Imperial War Museum North or enjoy some fine dining in the multitude of bars and restaurants.

32. GET SOME FRESH AIR

Not all the Manchester highlights are indoors. There's much to be seen and done if you want to stretch your legs. Although it's a concrete jungle, there are still plenty of lovely green spots scattered around the city.

Chorlton Waterpark is a lovely spot for an afternoon walk. Popular with joggers, cyclists and dog walkers, it's a great place to soak up the summer sun. You can't swim here nor hire boats, but don't be dismayed. There's a path that takes you from Chorlton Waterpark to the adjoining Sale Waterpark, where you can most definitely swim and hire boats.

The route between the 2 is a nice figure of eight, taking in lovely scenic views. It's around 6km and all relatively flat so it's suitable for all abilities.

Sale Waterpark run open-swim sessions, so you're safe knowing it's all supervised and secure. They also have facilities for changing and refreshments. If you want to have a little more action, try any number of the watersports on offer - stand up paddleboard, kayak or even jet skiing. I bet you didn't think I'd mention jet skis in a Manchester guide, right?

33. KEEP ON WALKING

If all that sounds like too much hard work, just keep on walking. Manchester is full of great long walks and trails. If you want to see the greener, calmer side of the city, lace up your boots and get walking.

The path between the 2 waterparks? That's actually part of a much bigger route. Keep on following and you'll eventually end up in Liverpool. If you've only got a few days in Manchester, that's not very practical, but it's handy to know.

Many of the routes follow the waterways and canals and can be the perfect antidote to city overload. The majority are well maintained and perfectly safe during the daytime. They're probably safe during the evening too, but if they're not well lit I wouldn't risk it.

The trails can also be used by cyclists, so if you prefer 2 wheels over 2 feet, get on your bike. If you are going by bike, double-check the route first. Some of the trails through the city centre may include one-way streets, and the more rural paths could get a little muddy. Spend a little time pre-planning to avoid any unwanted incidents.

34. A TRIP TO THE FOREST

While technically a little outside Manchester, a trip to Macclesfield would be a lovely addition to any itinerary if you're a fan of the outdoors. The town itself is quite small and quaint, but the real beauty comes when you get off the beaten track and head to the forest.

The Macclesfield Forest Circular is around 7km of moderate hiking. If you're lucky you'll see red deer and a multitude of birds. The nearby reservoirs attract all manner of wildlife, making it a perfect spot to relax and recharge the batteries.

If your batteries are fully charged and you want a challenge though, consider a hike from Macclesfield over to Lyme Park. It's another 7km trip, but this one has something very special along the route.

Lyme Park is the stately home featured in the 1995 BBC adaptation of Pride & Prejudice. It's a stunning building, and the grounds are pretty lovely too. It's free to walk around, and this trail takes in a good portion. If you need some fresh air, add this to your list.

35. SEE THE BBC

Back in the city centre, next to Salford Quays, is Media City - the home of the BBC. I was a little sceptical about how much fun a tour of a news headquarters could be, but I was nicely surprised. The old BBC headquarters (also in Manchester) was ugly and not very exciting. My expectations were low, but Media City is well worth exploring.

As it's a working site you'll get to see everything in real-time, plus the guide offers really interesting insights into both TV and Radio. The interactive elements are fun, and I guarantee you'll walk away with a greater appreciation of the production that goes into seemingly simple shows.

Another tour for TV lovers would be the Coronation Street tour. The world's longest-running soap opera (from December 1960), the tour takes place at Media City and takes you around the iconic set. Even if you've never watched a single episode (like me), you'll still likely recognise the backdrops.

36. CRYSTAL MAZE

Before Escape Rooms were a thing, there was Crystal Maze. A TV show from back in the 90s, teams would compete to solve puzzles and escape rooms. Atmospheric, tense and lots of fun. Nowadays Escape Rooms are everywhere, in every major city.

But what if you could go back and do the original? Not only puzzle solving, but challenges that test your physical prowess too? The more people complete their challenges, the more are available for the final group task of collecting gold tokens in a giant windswept crystal.

Trust me, it's amazing fun.

The whole experience lasts around 2 hours, so it's easy to fit into your schedule, and should hopefully provide some lasting Manchester memories.

While it's not the cheapest activity in the city, there are always plenty of discounts and coupon codes bouncing around the internet. It's located a minute away from The Science and Industry Museum too, so chain them together for the ultimate day out.

37. FESTIVAL SEASON

Time your visit to Manchester to coincide with one of many festivals to get the most bang for your buck. Most take place during the warmer summer months, but you can usually find something going on year-round.

Depending on your preference, check out MANIFF, MIF and Sound of the City.

MANIFF stands for Manchester International Film Festival, takes place during March and celebrates films and short pieces from across the globe. Not quite at the level of Cannes, it's still an excellent independent festival.

If you're a film buff, movie geek or cinephile, you'll be in your element as close to 200 screenings fill the week. For the ultra-dedicated, keep an eye out for the meet and greets and question times - actors, producers, casting directors. Get up close and dive deeper into the experience.

MIF is Manchester International Festival (not to be confused with MANIFF). MIF covers a wider spectrum of entertainment, performing arts and pop culture. Think modern art, stage performances and spoken word.

While that may sound a little artsy, MIF attracts some well-known celebrity figures. Previous attendees and performers include Yoko Ono, Idris Elba and filmmaker David Lynch. It's a huge operation spanning the entire city centre. Download the official app, create your schedule and enjoy the July sunshine as you wander from performance to performance.

Sound of the City is a music festival based in Castlefield, on the old Roman site. Massive international acts descend on the city - Kylie Minogue, Arcade Fire, Blink 182. The performances are open-air yet still intimate, with a limited capacity of just over 8000, while the unusual surroundings just add to the spectacle.

38. SO MANY WALKING TOURS

If big crowds aren't your thing and you want a peaceful introduction to the city, walking tours are always an option. They run throughout the year and cover all manner of topics and angles.

Some are your classic architecture, history and general background tours. Others focus on the music scene, highlighting key venues, landmarks and musical hotspots. Then there's the street art, food (called the Scranchester Tour - Scran being a casual word for food) and my favourite, the craft beer tours.

Everyone has different hobbies and passions, and you can likely find a tour to scratch that itch. Lots are free with donations happily accepted by the guides, while others require pre-booking. Shop around, check the reviews and choose one that interests you. There's a lifetime of history just waiting to be discovered.

39. PUB CRAWL - PRINTWORKS & CORN EXCHANGE

No Manchester guide would be complete without a pub crawl or two. It's a classic Manchester pastime. With over 650 licensed premises in the city centre, it'd be impossible to discuss (or visit) them all, so I'll narrow it down to a few key areas.

If you're thirsty in the city centre, it's a no brainer to visit the Printworks and Corn Exchange. Located adjacent to the Arndale shopping centre, you've already got more bars, pubs and cocktail venues than one could visit in a single sitting.

The Printworks is a leisure and entertainment complex, featuring a cinema, gym, escape room and a multitude of bars and restaurants. There's a selection for all palates, with diverse brands such as Walkabout, Wagamama and Hard Rock Cafe, all under one roof.

The atmosphere can get quite lively but, on the whole, it's a decent place for an evening out. If you want a little more sophistication, head across the street to the Corn Exchange.

If you hear a local refer to The Triangle, don't be confused. It's the same thing. Originally named the Corn and Produce Exchange, it was a commerce hub of the early 1900s. Until 1996 it was a bohemian dream, housing local designers, memorabilia stalls and tattoo artists. The IRA bombing destroyed most of that.

It was rebuilt into a shiny retail outlet (named The Triangle), before reverting to the original name and becoming the current leisure hub of restaurants, bars and a very fancy hotel.

If the Printworks is a pint of beer, the Corn Exchange would be a glass of Pimms. Each to their own.

40. PUB CRAWL – SINCLAIR'S OYSTER BAR

While in sight of the Printworks and Corn Exchange, I feel the Oyster Bar deserves its own entry. From the iconic look, feel and design to the unrivalled atmosphere, you must add it to your list.

Found in Shambles Square, the Oyster Bar forms a horseshoe of pubs with The Old Wellington Inn and The Mitre Hotel (with Manchester Cathedral sitting right behind). In the middle of that horseshoe lives a beer garden of joy, happiness and one or two headaches.

On a sunny day, there's nowhere finer in the whole of the city. The large round outdoor tables encourage mingling and mixing, leading to new friendships and hot debates sprouting all night long.

While the other 2 pubs are nice and well worth visiting (The Wellington Inn being the only surviving Tudor building in Manchester), Sinclair's is a different beast. Originally located across town, in the early 1970s, it was transported wholesale to the current location.

The white walls with exposed beams, the deceptively low ceilings, and the snug little corners and tiny rooms all add to the magic. As it's a Sam Smith's pub, they also don't serve the commercial beers you find in every other bar and pub. You either get an

Ale, Lager, Stout or Cider. Nice and simple, but very tasty and very reasonably priced.

41. PUB CRAWL – UNUSUAL BARS

- Twenty Twenty Two

- Alcotraz

- Flight Club Manchester

If you're looking for something a little extra with your frosty beverage, Manchester is home to quite a few weird and wonderful establishments.

Who knew ping pong and beer would go together? While beer pong is a classic student activity, Twenty Twenty Two adds a little class to the mix. Situated on Little Lever Street in the Northern Quarter, TTT combines a classic drinking establishment with table tennis and loud music.

If you're serious about your paddle sports, it fills up fast so get in early. Also keep your spidey sense on standby as rogue balls do have a habit of whizzing by as the night goes on. That all takes place in the back though, so you can enjoy some of the drinks deals and banging music without fear of being struck.

Alcotraz has a different spin, taking inspiration from the famous American prison. 'A prison-themed cocktail experience', you 'smuggle' in your own booze for the 'inmates' to mix for you... all while sitting in your cell wearing an orange jumpsuit. It may be a little convoluted and performance for some, but it'll certainly be a story to tell the grandkids (and great material for your social feed).

Flight Club Manchester goes back to the sports theme, but this time bringing the classic pub game of darts into the 21st century. Darts, for those who've never played, involves throwing 3 sharp little darts at a circular corkboard, attempting to get the highest score possible.

Flight Club adds some tech to remove the burden of adding and multiplying, which can be tricky after a few pints. The energy in the room is awesome and it's just a great place to hang out. If you're after unusual yet fun, this gets my vote.

42. PUB CRAWL – JOIN THE RAIL ALE TRAIL

If you're too lazy to walk between pubs or just want to combine your sightseeing and drinking, try an ale trail. This usually involves hopping on and off a train or Metrolink, and sampling a delicious beverage at each stop.

The East Lancashire Railway run an excellent trail, through stunning towns and villages. The train ticket and a complimentary bottle of ale are provided, then you're guided off and on as you explore the quaint old pubs along the route.

Alternatively, you can create your own trail - a popular one being the Metrolink from Bury to Manchester, hopping off and on along the way for a frosty beverage. Unlike the organised tours, you won't be regaled with history and local wisdom along the way, but you have a little more freedom to explore.

As with all transport in Manchester, a valid ticket is required. Don't try and travel without paying as the fines can be huge and are completely unnecessary. Ticket Inspectors are common, so don't risk it. Get a Daysaver ticket and take as many trips as you want.

43. PUB CRAWL – THE GAY VILLAGE

Not so much a pub crawl as a tour of an iconic area of Manchester. Nestled alongside the Rochdale Canal, Canal Street is the centre of Manchester's thriving gay community. On a sunny evening the cobbled street comes alive as people spill out of the bars and clubs to continue the party.

While Manchester Pride Festival comes around once a year in late August, the Village is a hotspot of music, celebrations and parties all year round.

There's a wide selection of venues ranging from quiet old pubs to pop camp classics, you'll find something going on 7 nights a week.

It's inclusive, welcoming and a right good time. Add it to your list.

44. WHERE TO STAY

While there are plenty of nice areas to stay in around Manchester, if time's against you then I'd choose the city centre every time.

Travelodge, Premier Inn and Ibis are all very reasonable for a long weekend, usually coming in below £50. They're clean, usually in easy to find locations and the staff are great.

If money's no object then the sky's the limit. Most visiting celebrities tend to stay in the Lowry Hotel, where you can spend upwards of £400 per night.

There's truly no shortage of places to stay in the city centre.

45. GETTING AROUND – TAXI TOUR

Who in the city knows everything? Who talks to everyone and soaks in information like a sponge? Taxi drivers. So who better to give you a tour of that very same city?

There's one in Manchester, he goes by the name of John Consterdine and he's a bit of a local legend. He's acquired a lifetime of knowledge of the city and loves to share it with his passengers. Running bespoke and specialised tours, he can blow your mind with the knowledge he brings.

If you've got a particular interest - music, architecture, history, let him know and he tailors the tour to suit. A proud Mancunian born and bred, he's also just a lovely bloke.

With an almost clean sweep of 5 stars on Trip Advisor, Manchester Taxi Tours could be the tipping point that pushes your trip from great to outstanding.

46. GETTING AROUND – FREE BUS

This was something I was completely unaware of until recently! I had no idea this was a thing.

It's a hop-on, hop-off bus that runs every 10 minutes. They loop around the city, taking in all the main areas and attractions, and you don't pay a penny. Look for the giant yellow bus with Free Bus Around The City in the window. They're not hard to spot.

While Manchester is definitely a walkable city centre, if time isn't on your side it can be wise to jump on the free bus. You'll miss some of the magic from exploring by foot, but they're safe, reliable and free. It's hard to argue with that.

They run from 7 am until 10 pm, so check them out.

47. GETTING AROUND – METROLINK

While I've mentioned the Metrolink several times already, it is worth getting its own shoutout. It's neither the cheapest nor fastest mode of transport around, but it's fairly reliable and the network covers a big chunk of the city.

While I recommend it for casual use due to the ease and connectivity, when there are issues, there are issues. Lines close down, alternative bus routes which take a lifetime are put on, or they just close and you're stuck.

Always have a backup plan, and that plan should be Uber or some other taxi app. Unless you're travelling long distances, to the airport for example, Uber is fine. If you are going to the airport from the town centre, the train is quick, cheap and very reliable.

At peak times the Metrolink (or tram as it's often called) can get crazy busy and you either squeeze on or gamble and wait for the next. It's by no means a terrible system. I love the Metrolink, but I've been stranded more times than I'd care to remember and forced to either take a very long bus or taxi.

48. DAY TRIPS

If you've seen and done everything and have some time to spare, consider a day trip. Manchester's a great hub, with plenty of great options within a short distance.

The biggest one would be Liverpool. In just over an hour on the train you're in the heart of Merseyside. Tickets are crazy cheap if booked in advance, so consider piggybacking your love of the Beatles onto your Manchester experience.

Head South West for an hour on the train and you're in Chester. It's a photographers dream with the medieval architecture and picturesque surroundings.

Both the Lake District and Peak District are just over an hour away and both are jaw-droppingly beautiful. Think of a mini New Zealand, with the rolling green hills and epic lakes. If hiking's your thing and you're sick of the big city, lace up your boots and visit Kinder Scout or Lake Windermere. If you don't fall in love with them, I question if your heart is still beating.

49. LOOK TO THE STARS

If you're looking for unique experiences, add Jodrell Bank to your itinerary. It's not every day you get to visit a UNESCO World Heritage site, and especially not when it's a giant space telescope!

For over 50 years the Lovell Telescope has studied the mysteries of the universe, and it's right on our doorstep. You don't have to climb a mountain to get there or sail out into the Pacific. Just jump on a train for 40 minutes.

Aside from the giant telescope, there are interactive elements, exhibitions and daily talks. What they also do, which I think is amazing, is host open-air concerts. Giant displays are beamed onto the disk, creating epic light shows and the perfect backdrop to shake your bootie. Bands like The Flaming Lips and OK GO have performed there, with hopefully more coming in the future. If you get to see a gig there, you've succeeded at life. Congratulations.

50. WHAT'S WITH ALL THE BEES?

As you've been wandering around the city, exploring and observing, you may have noticed an abundance of bees. Across the whole city, in all the corners, you'll find street art and murals of the humble worker bee. Why? Because it's the symbol of Manchester.

Back during the Industrial Revolution is was commented that the endless hordes of workers pouring into the cotton factories resembles worker bees. It stuck. They're even featured in the crest of the city's arms.

So beloved have the bees become, that countless exhibitions, competitions and displays have been made to honour them. For a time there were 101 giant colourful bee statues displayed across the city. They were like Pokemon… you had to follow the trail and catch them all.

They were later auctioned off, raising over £1Million for charity, but there are still plenty of murals and graffiti to find.

The humble bee symbolises hard work, determination and industriousness. I think that's a fitting symbol for this beautiful city.

BONUS TIPS –

1. HONEST ABE IN MANCHESTER

Are you aware that Manchester played a pivotal role in ending the American Civil War? Abe Lincoln even wrote to the humble Manchester worker to thank them.

Manchester was the centre of the Industrial Revolution due to the textile mills and the distribution via the canal system. Manchester was importing millions of lbs of cotton to feed the machines, but the majority of that cotton was coming from slave plantations in the US south.

Fortunes were being made and people were prospering, but the mill workers decided the price was too high. They refused to work with cotton picked on the plantations. This principled stand financially crippled the plantation owners, allowing Abe to win the battle and thus leading to the abolition of slavery.

A statue of Mr Lincoln still stands in Lincoln Square, a testament to the integrity and power of the people.

2. ALIENS HAVE LANDED

If that last one was a little heavy, let's lighten the mood by talking about space invaders.

Remember the alien characters in Space Invaders on the arcade machines and later Atari 2600? The blocky things that inched down the screen, pixel by pixel, until you shot them with your little brick at the bottom of the screen?

Those thing? They're all over the city. A French artist created 47 mosaic tile pieces and positioned them in random locations around the city. I've personally found a few in the Northern Quarter, and one by the Cathedral, but I never found them all.

Time (and redevelopment) hasn't been kind, and some are starting to fade or crumble completely, but it's still a fun Easter Egg hunt. He's placed them all over the world, so keep an eye out the next time you hit the road. Check out space-invaders.com for more details.

TOP REASONS TO BOOK THIS TRIP

History: Manchester's been at the centre of so many global milestones. Never let it be forgotten

Music: If you love music, you'll never be bored

Variety: In the space of 24hrs you could be dancing in a Roman fort, kayaking across a water park and drinking cocktails in a prison cell. Sounds fun, right?

PACKING AND PLANNING TIPS

A Week before Leaving

- Arrange for someone to take care of pets and water plants.

- Email and Print important Documents.

- Get Visa and vaccines if needed.

- Check for travel warnings.

- Stop mail and newspaper.

- Notify Credit Card companies where you are going.

- Passports and photo identification is up to date.

- Pay bills.

- Copy important items and download travel Apps.

- Start collecting small bills for tips.

- Have post office hold mail while you are away.

- Check weather for the week.

- Car inspected, oil is changed, and tires have the correct pressure.

- Check airline luggage restrictions.

- Download Apps needed for your trip.

Right Before Leaving

- Contact bank and credit cards to tell them your location.

- Clean out refrigerator.

- Empty garbage cans.

- Lock windows.

- Make sure you have the proper identification with you.

- Bring cash for tips.

- Remember travel documents.

- Lock door behind you.

- Remember wallet.

- Unplug items in house and pack chargers.

- Change your thermostat settings.

- Charge electronics, and prepare camera memory cards.

READ OTHER
GREATER THAN A TOURIST
BOOKS

Greater Than a Tourist- California: 50 Travel Tips from Locals

Greater Than a Tourist- Salem Massachusetts USA50 Travel Tips from a Local by Danielle Lasher

Greater Than a Tourist United States: 50 Travel Tips from Locals

Greater Than a Tourist- St. Croix US Birgin Islands USA: 50 Travel Tips from a Local by Tracy Birdsall

Greater Than a Tourist- Montana: 50 Travel Tips from a Local by Laurie White

Children's Book: Charlie the Cavalier Travels the World by Lisa Rusczyk Ed. D.

> TOURIST

Follow us on Instagram for beautiful travel images:
http://Instagram.com/GreaterThanATourist

Follow *Greater Than a Tourist* on Amazon.

CZYKPublishing.com

> TOURIST

At *Greater Than a Tourist*, we love to share travel tips with you. How did we do? What guidance do you have for how we can give you better advice for your next trip? Please send your feedback to GreaterThanaTourist@gmail.com as we continue to improve the series. We appreciate your constructive feedback. Thank you.

METRIC CONVERSIONS

TEMPERATURE

110° F — — 40° C
100° F —
90° F — — 30° C
80° F —
70° F — — 20° C
60° F —
50° F — — 10° C
40° F —
32° F — — 0° C
20° F —
10° F — — -10° C
0° F —
-10° F — — -18° C
-20° F — — -30° C

To convert F to C:

Subtract 32, and then multiply by 5/9 or .5555.

To Convert C to F:

Multiply by 1.8 and then add 32.

32F = 0C

LIQUID VOLUME

To Convert:................Multiply by
U.S. Gallons to Liters............... 3.8
U.S. Liters to Gallons 26
Imperial Gallons to U.S. Gallons 1.2
Imperial Gallons to Liters....... 4.55
Liters to Imperial Gallons 22
1 Liter = .26 U.S. Gallon
1 U.S. Gallon = 3.8 Liters

DISTANCE

To convert ....Multiply by
Inches to Centimeters 2.54
Centimeters to Inches 39
Feet to Meters...................... .3
Meters to Feet 3.28
Yards to Meters 91
Meters to Yards 1.09
Miles to Kilometers 1.61
Kilometers to Miles............ .62
1 Mile = 1.6 km
1 km = .62 Miles

WEIGHT

1 Ounce = .28 Grams
1 Pound = .4555 Kilograms
1 Gram = .04 Ounce
1 Kilogram = 2.2 Pounds

TRAVEL QUESTIONS

- Do you bring presents home to family or friends after a vacation?

- Do you get motion sick?

- Do you have a favorite billboard?

- Do you know what to do if there is a flat tire?

- Do you like a sun roof open?

- Do you like to eat in the car?

- Do you like to wear sun glasses in the car?

- Do you like toppings on your ice cream?

- Do you use public bathrooms?

- Did you bring a cell phone and does it have power?

- Do you have a form of identification with you?

- Have you ever been pulled over by a cop?

- Have you ever given money to a stranger on a road trip?

- Have you ever taken a road trip with animals?

- Have you ever gone on a vacation alone?

- Have you ever run out of gas?

- If you could move to any place in the world, where would it be?

- If you could travel anywhere in the world, where would you travel?

- If you could travel in any vehicle, which one would it be?

- If you had three things to wish for from a magic genie, what would they be?

- If you have a driver's license, how many times did it take you to pass the test?

- What are you the most afraid of on vacation?

- What do you want to get away from the most when you are on vacation?

- What foods smell bad to you?

- What item do you bring on ever trip with you away from home?

- What makes you sleepy?

- What song would you love to hear on the radio when you're cruising on the highway?

- What travel job would you want the least?

- What will you miss most while you are away from home?

- What is something you always wanted to try?

- What is the best road side attraction that you ever saw?

- What is the farthest distance you ever biked?

- What is the farthest distance you ever walked?

- What is the weirdest thing you needed to buy while on vacation?

- What is your favorite candy?

- What is your favorite color car?

- What is your favorite family vacation?

- What is your favorite food?

- What is your favorite gas station drink or food?

- What is your favorite license plate design?

- What is your favorite restaurant?

- What is your favorite smell?

- What is your favorite song?

- What is your favorite sound that nature makes?

- What is your favorite thing to bring home from a vacation?

- What is your favorite vacation with friends?

- What is your favorite way to relax?

- Where is the farthest place you ever traveled in a car?

- Where is the farthest place you ever went North, South, East and West?

- Where is your favorite place in the world?

- Who is your favorite singer?

- Who taught you how to drive?

- Who will you miss the most while you are away?

- Who if the first person you will contact when you get to your destination?

- Who brought you on your first vacation?

- Who likes to travel the most in your life?

- Would you rather be hot or cold?

- Would you rather drive above, below, or at the speed limited?

- Would you rather drive on a highway or a back road?

- Would you rather go on a train or a boat?

- Would you rather go to the beach or the woods?

TRAVEL BUCKET LIST

1.

2.

3.

4.

5.

6.

7.

8.

9.

10.

NOTES

Made in the USA
Monee, IL
28 December 2024

75511706R00056